A Life

Beyond ~~ABUSE~~

Jerhonda Pace

W9-ASA-386

Pacers

We are a team.

I love you all beyond words.

My life is better because of each one of you.

One

I was born and semi-raised in Chicago, I spent the first 9 years of my life in Chicago. I lived all over Chicago before my mom moved us off to the Northwest suburbs of Chicago- Streamwood, that's where we ended up living. Spring of 1997, I was 4-years-old, we were living in Henry Horner Homes which is a housing project in Chicago on the west side, for those of you who are unfamiliar with the housing projects, it was the ghetto, there is no other way to put it. Our neighborhood was filled with gang violence, drug dealing, random daylight shootings, robberies, and theft. At any moment you could become a victim of some form of violence, no exaggeration. It was best for kids to remain in the house after sundown. Cops didn't care to get involved when it came to crime prevention, in fact, some police were a part of the problem, they were helping the drug dealers by being the lookout, they kept them informed about upcoming drug raids. One spring evening, my mom decided that she didn't feel like cooking and thought that restaurant food would be faster. My mom, my older brother, and other sister headed out to the restaurant while I stayed back with my mother's cousin.

4-year-old me would have slowed my pregnant mother down, it wasn't out of the ordinary for me to stay inside, especially when they were going to be walking after sundown. After left out, I sat on the floor in front of the floor model TV- watching Beavis and Butt-Head. I knew they wouldn't be gone long, the restaurant was close to our second-floor apartment. You could look out the window in our living room and see the restaurant, it was just that close. My mother's cousin came from the bedroom to the living room, stood in front of me and turned the TV off and said, "come back here, so I can watch you." I followed him to the bedroom, his girlfriend was laying in the bed when we walked in. My mother's cousin climbed onto the bed, moved over to the middle of the bed, then told me to follow. I climbed onto the bed as I was told. Once I was in the bed, he put the blanket over us and cuddled me in a spooning position. He lifted my Barbie nightgown and put his hand in my panties and fondled me. He inserted his finger in my vagina as I cried and attempted to close my legs and wiggle from under his grip. I said "that hurt" but that didn't stop him from continuing. His girlfriend got out of the bed and left the room as if she knew exactly what was going on, I just knew she was going to come back and save me, she never returned. When he decided to stop, he got out of the bed and left the room. I laid there, in silence, scared to move. A few minutes later he came back for me. I wasn't sure what to expect. He took me in the bathroom, grabbed a washcloth, wet it with warm water then wiped my vagina off. After her cleaned me up, he put Vaseline on my vagina and butt. Right when my mother, brother, and sister walked in, he was pulling my gown down. He rushed me out the bathroom and lied to my mother by saying that I had peed on myself, so he cleaned me up.

That's where it all began.

Two

Living in the Chicago projects wasn't all that bad to me as a kid. Thanks to the local drug dealers and gangbangers, I learned about crime early on. I've witnessed people do drugs and sell them. My family was caught up in the illegal drug industry both ways: some were either using drugs or selling drugs. Yes, the projects were unsafe, but it was home to me, it was all that I knew. In fact, it was home to a lot of the kids that I grew up with, we all came from the same struggle. Summers there was the absolute best. Every summer one of the local drug dealers would use a monkey ranch to remove the cap from the fire hydrant and all of us kids would be out there having the time of our lives playing in the water. Our playground didn't consist of much, just a few medal slides, and swings that were broken. I didn't understand how someone could break a swing, but the seats of the swings were always missing. On nice days we could go to the playground while some of the adults would sit on milk crates in front of the building smoking weed and cigarettes, quenching their thirst with a 40oz bottle of beer. The other adults would be closer to the playground, barbequing on the built-in barbecue grills. Summer nights always ended with my grandmother calling my name from her 5th-floor apartment, that was the norm. Children were always watched, no matter what. It wasn't uncommon for someone like my grandmother to be watching the kids at the playground. Of course, I was teased on the playground whenever my grandmother called me- I was known as the "early bird" since I wasn't allowed to stay out longer. The truth is: I wanted to stay out longer, but dinner was always at 5 PM, after dinner I sat in a chair at the same window that my grandmother sat in, but this time I was the one watching the kids play before the moon replaced the sun in the sky. Once everyone went inside for the night, I would read a book (mainly look at the pictures and make up my own stories to match the photos). This became my nightly routine, after my sexual abuse experience; most of my days were spent upstairs inside my grandmother's apartment. I never told my grandmother what happened to me, I didn't even tell my father. I told my sister and my mom about what happened, but I was ignored. Once I was ignored, that made me shut down and not want to speak of the sexual abuse again. That was the start of my silence.

Three

We moved from the projects shortly after my 5th birthday. When we were packing our bags, getting ready to leave the only place I knew as home. During our packing my mother was happy, I'd never seen my mother so happy, she was truly happy; maybe it was the change of scenery for her or it could have been making it out of the projects that made her so happy, but it was something that I know made her smile from ear to ear. Even though I was a part of the move, I didn't stay long. I ended up living with my grandmother and finishing out my Kindergarten year at Brown school. I wanted to stay with my grandmother and I was excited when it happened. I would go home every weekend to be with my mother and siblings. It was convenient because we didn't move too far out, in-fact, we still lived on the west side of Chicago, we just moved near Mount Sanai Hospital. That's where my mother met her then lover, Big Man. They dated for a little while, once their relationship became serious, we ended up moving again. . . Even though I didn't stay at our apartment long, I was only there on weekends, I was excited about our new move. There were only 4 of us at the time; my older sister who is 6 years older than me, my older brother who is 3 years older than me and my younger sister who is 4 years younger than me. When we moved to our apartment on Springfield, I was 6-years-old I had graduated kindergarten and I was back with my mother and siblings full-time. Life was great for me, I was happy about everything that was happening. We hadn't been living on Springfield for two weeks before I made new friends. Living on Springfield was so different, it was like a whole new world. There were no projects, all the houses were nice historic brick homes, around the corner were brownstones, the people were nice, the neighbors were like family, everything was perfect. My brother and I used to hang out a lot, I was the annoying little sister who wanted to be tough and hang out with the big boys, therefore I was always tagging along. Whenever you saw my brother, I wasn't too far behind. One day we were walking to the candy store lady house to get Flamin' Hot with cheese and meat on it, pickles with peppermints & Kool-Aid, and ice cups, which is frozen Kool-Aid in a styrofoam cup. On our way back from the store we met our soon-to-been friends. They were brother and sister, just like us. We were the same age, but my brother was two years younger than her brother. We all started hanging out, regularly especially during the summer months. We all grew closer over time. One day my brother and I asked my mom if it was okay for us to spend the night at our friends' house. My mom was okay with us staying over, our moms had met, and we were with each other daily, we even did our homework together on school days, before dinner. Our apartments were close, we lived around the corner from one another, on top of that, my mom's old friend was their neighbor, so that made my mother's decision a lot easier. She was comfortable allowing us to stay over and we were comfortable staying over. The night of us sleeping over was supposed to be a good one but turned into something totally different. My brother and I were at our friends' house getting ready for bed. My friend and I were in the room, talking about downtown- they had never been to downtown Chicago. I remember just describing it was a place full of big buildings and telling her about how we go downtown every year, during Christmas season to take pictures with Santa. Our brothers were in the living room playing a game on the Nintendo 64. Bedtime came around and my brother decided that he was no longer spending the night, he ended up leaving, I stayed there. I wanted to continue with the sleepover. My brother was a true homebody, so I wasn't surprised by his decision. My friend and I laid down in her bed, she gave me my own blanket and we slept head to foot in her bed. Her brother came into the room and got into the other bed. They shared a room together. We had been sleeping for only an hour or so, when her brother suddenly got into the bed with us, awakening me. He laid behind me and started rubbing on my thigh. I pushed him and told him not to touch me. He told me to "shut up" and continued to force himself on me. This was all too familiar to me, I knew this was a battle that I would lose, so I didn't fight, I just started crying and hoped that it would be over soon. He put his hand over my mouth as he used his other hand to pull my pajama pants down. He licked his hand and touched himself before I knew it he was penetrating my anus with his penis and all I could do was cry as he tightened his grip on my mouth, causing me to bite my tongue. I just wanted everything to be over at that point. I thought it would never end until finally, he stopped. He pulled himself together and got back in his own bed. My friend never woke up, she slept through everything. I didn't go back to sleep afterward, I stayed up silently crying. The next day, her mother made breakfast; sausages, eggs, and toast. We sat at the table together, my friend, her brother, and their mother. I didn't eat my food. I said I wasn't hungry, but I did drink the Kool-Aid. Their mother sat down long enough to eat her toast, then she went to shower.

Once she left the table my friend's brother smiled at me, then went into the living room. I put my head down and looked away. He got up from the table and went to play his game. My friend looked at me, then asked me "Did he touch you?" I didn't answer her question. My eyes started to water, then she stated: "I know he did, he always do that". She didn't seem shocked, she seemed more annoyed than anything as if this was the norm and she was tired of him doing it to everybody. I got up and told her "He touched me. . . I'm leaving." I left out the door and I ran home. I never spoke to them again. I had yet another secret to keep.

Four

Moving day. . . AGAIN! The time had come for us to move
from our apartment on Springfield to an apartment on
Lockwood. This was by far the most exciting move for me.
I knew we would be moving into the building next to my
auntie building and I was so happy about that. My aunt's
daughter and I were favorite cousins. We were not blood
cousins, but our moms were best-friends and called each
other sisters, therefore we were raised knowing one another
as cousins. I didn't make many friends during our brief stay
at this apartment, I didn't want to make friends, then leave
them, which happened often for me. Instead, I decided to
stick to who I knew and spend my days with my cousin. I
was invited to my cousin's birthday party at their
apartment. When my mom gave me to okay to go to my
cousin's birthday party/slumber party, I immediately ran
into my room and packed my overnight bag. Even though I
wasn't going far, I wanted to take my bag with me, it was
mandatory since I was going to be spending the night out.
The party started at 3 PM. My mom walked me and my
younger sister over to her building around 2:30 PM- yes, I
was one of those kids who showed up to events on time. As

a kid, I was never late for anything, my mom made sure that we were early so that we would be on time for everything that we could possibly be involved in. When I arrived at my cousin's house my auntie had the hotdogs boiling, individual bags of chips on the table and a pitcher of strawberry Kool-Aid was in the freezer- it was time to party. Before I could even grab a bag of chips she made sure I understood the rules: "Don't be running in my house. Make sure y'all wash ya' hands before y'all touch anything. I don't want to hear no arguing about who sleeping where. Don't drink all my Kool-Aid. The minute one of y'all do something, all of y'all goin' ta bed." My only response was "Okay auntie" then I ran into my cousin's room to let her know that I was ready to party. Partying for us was playing in my auntie's makeup, putting on her heels, and taking pictures. We always used up the film in my aunt's Polaroid camera. In our mind we were models. As we were playing, there was a knock at the door, more party guest was arriving. I heard my auntie repeating the rules to the other kids. There was three of them. After she repeated the rules, my mom came into the room to let me know that she was leaving and had put my bag on the couch. Right after she left my auntie called for us to come to eat. My cousin and I kicked my aunt's shoes off and raced to the kitchen. She completely disregarded the fact that she had other guests there. Whenever my cousin and I were together, we were inseparable. We all sat on the floor in the living room eating our hot dogs and chips, the Kool-Aid wasn't cold, so we had to drink water. When we were done eating we had a dance contest, played musical chairs, and watched a movie. Time flew by, before we knew it, it was time to go to sleep. Two of the party guest didn't spend the night, they ended up leaving before we went to sleep. We slept on the floor in the living room. When we laid down, I wasn't sleepy, so I laid there, in the dark. My cousin's God-sister was in the middle of us. She was much old than we were, I was 8-years-old at the time and her God-sister was 13-years-old. My aunt was her Godmother, so she came around quite often. That night everything changed. While my cousin was sleeping, her God-sister turned my way and put her hand under my shirt, I pushed her hand away and told her to stop, she said, "Be quiet, you're going to like it", I didn't say anything else, I knew from experience that saying something or trying to fight a person off you wouldn't make that person stop. I laid there, in silence- as she had her way with me. She performed sexual acts on me orally and with her fingers. When she was done, I was sworn into secrecy, as if I was going to tell. I knew that nobody would believe me, I wasn't believed the first time it happened. Nothing was done about my previous sexual abuse, so I knew this time would be no different, this was just another one for the books.

Five

After I watched my mother go through another failed relationship, it was time to move again. This time we ended up moving to the south side. We moved to a house on 120th Place out in the Roseland neighborhood. Moving to the south side was blah, I wasn't too excited, but I wasn't sad either. Our family grew, I had a new little sister whom I loved and adored. My other siblings didn't really care about the move. My oldest sister was just ready to settle down and stop moving around so much. We moved in at night, my youngest sister's father helping us. We all had our own dad's. Even though my mother's relationship didn't last with him, he still came around from time to time. The reason for our night move was that my mother never wanted anyone to see what she's bringing into her house. After settling in, we all went to sleep. Literally, the next day- there was a knock on the door, which my older sister answered. There were three girls standing there that asked, "Is there anybody here that play double-dutch?" my sister called me to the front and asked me "Do you wanna jump rope with them?" I didn't have anything going on at the time so I said "Yeah". My sister sat on the porch and watched us jump rope. We all talked about where we're from and what we wanted to be when we grew up. They gave me insight on the neighborhood and told me which school they went to, even telling me which houses on the block had kids around our ages that I could play with since we were all the same age. They were nice girls and eventually, we all became good friends. We started hanging out regularly. We lived on the south side for a few years. Early in 2003 around late February or early March, my mother and brother came home with R. Kelly's Chocolate Factory CD. My sister who was an R. Kelly fan played that CD every day, no exaggeration. Our upstairs neighbors were always playing R. Kelly's R. CD as well. I remember walking around outside and hearing people playing R. Kelly's music from their cars. Whenever we went to family parties, gatherings, and family reunions, R. Kelly's music was being played. Being surrounded by his music, I became a fan. I started listening to his music just as much, if not more than the people around me. I liked all of his music. As my mother's relationships diminished, I found myself escaping to R. Kelly's music more. Whenever I was having a bad day, I would listen to his music. It always seemed to change my mood for the better. Music and writing became my life. I found myself writing poetry, my topics being music and life. I kept a journal near and always wrote in it. Things had slightly begun to look up, though still, I was careful not to become too comfortable, because ultimately- the next year- we moved again.

Six

February of 2004- it was that time again. This wasn't going to be a move that we were used to, this time was different. We were moving out of Chicago, to the suburbs: Streamwood to be exact. I was angry about the move to Streamwood. I didn't know what to expect from the suburbs and I was tired of not having stability. Every time I was comfortable in school and made friends, it was time to move. I was 10-years-old, the school hadn't let out for the summer yet, which meant I had to start a new school a few months before school was out and make new friends. Plus, I was moving away from my grandma. My older sister was nearing 17, my older brother was almost 13, and I had 3 siblings under me ages 6, 3, and 1. We were all tired of moving. I was looking forward to the 1-hour drive though. This was our first day-light move, due to my mother's normal night move routine. Once we made it to the suburbs, I wasn't angry anymore. The neighborhood was beautiful, the grass was green- not a patch of brown grass or dirt in sight. There was a real park to go to, one that had working swings. We moved to a townhouse around the corner from that park. My mom was pointing everything out in the neighborhood as we were riding. When we pulled up to the house, my brother and I raced inside to pick our rooms. We knew that my mom would get the biggest room. We thought we would argue over who gets what room, but it was the complete opposite. We didn't argue at all. My brother picked the room that was closer to my mom. I didn't want that room anyways. I wanted the room that was near the top of the stairs. My other siblings didn't care about picking rooms. It was always my brother and me in competition over everything. That's how we bonded though. Ultimately, my brother is the reason why I have tough skin. Looking out of our mom's room window and watching the movers unload the moving truck, I knew every single last one of us were happy to be in the suburbs.

School for us started in the spring. I was nervous on my first day. I didn't know what to expect. My brother and I went to different schools. I went to elementary school and he went to middle school. We had never heard of that kind of separation before. On my first day of school, it was different. There were only five black kids, myself included. In Chicago, we went to majority black schools, so this was something completely different than what I was used to. My teacher was nice though, so it didn't take long for me to like my new school. Reality hit me when we had a talk about our families and our plans for the summer. That's when I knew something was different about me. All the kids in my class were talking about how their parents were married, they talked about their siblings and vacation. My parents weren't married, I had more siblings than everyone in the classroom, and my vacation was always spent at grandma's house. When school was out, I wanted to rush home and question my mom. Instead, I listened to R. Kelly's music and did some writing. I had the average black kid in Chicago story. I was always able to relate to kids in Chicago. My dad wasn't involved in my life, he spent most of his days incarcerated so my grandma and my aunt tried to make up for lost time with me on his behalf. My mother was always going through bad relationships, at the time she was no longer with my younger brother and sister dad, she was back with my 6-year-old sister's dad. I didn't understand why my mother didn't have a stable relationship or why my father couldn't stay out of prison. I blamed myself for my parents failed relationship. I thought maybe if I hadn't come along things would have been better between them. The fact that I didn't have my dad in my life, it made me envious of the kids who had their dad around. We had this big recital coming up, it was right before school let out for the summer. I could be a part of it even though I started school late. My music teacher said I could join in, only if I learned the songs in time. I learned the songs and I was ready to sing. On the night of the recital, my classmates had their families show up to watch them perform and they were excited. I looked around and I had no one there to watch me perform. It seemed as if everyone's family made time for their special day, but my family couldn't make it. I noticed there was another girl whose family didn't show up. We were standing next to one another on stage. When the show was over, we talked for a little bit, then we walked home together. She lived a few minutes away from me on the other side of the park. We started hanging out more, sharing secrets, and bonding. Over time she became a sister to me. She was one year older than I was, and we had a lot in common. We were both from Chicago, raised in some of the toughest neighborhoods. I made a few more friends before summer vacation, so I had people to hang out with until I went to my grandma's house.

Seven

The next few years flew by with ease. I made more friends,
I was doing good in school, I was on a good path despite
the trauma that I suffered, years earlier. Even though my
life seemed to have been going in the right direction, there
was still a void that needed to be filled. I was still
communicating with my dad via letters to prison. I needed
my dad in my life and he wasn't there for me. There were
lots of broken promises and unanswered questions. I hated
my dad for not being there and I hated my mom for
allowing him to be absent, but I loved my mom so much
for making everything happen on her own, she was such a
strong woman- she was raising 6 kids on her own, I
admired her strength, but there were some things she just
couldn't teach me. I needed a solid foundation, I never had
that. Even though I had my father's side of the family in
my life, they couldn't replace him. Not only did I not have
my father growing up, I was left with bitter memories of
my dad. He was in and out of prison, never staying around
long enough for us to bond. It seemed as if he only came
around when he wanted to whoop me. That created
problems for me and I didn't bond with my dad the way

that I should have, I was hurt by his actions and I didn't understand his parenting. Perfect example: my dad was best friends with my uncle (my mother's brother). One day when I was 4-years-old we were over my uncle's house on the south side when my mother's cousin came over, who just so happened to be the same man who had sexually abused me months earlier. My dad didn't know about what happened to me, so when he told me to come over to say hi to him, I walked over to him and spit on him. I didn't want to be around him. My dad grabbed me by the arm, took me upstairs to the bathroom, pulled his brown leather belt off and whooped my butt, literally. He was holding me by one arm, I was screaming to the top of my lungs, running in what I thought was circles though, in reality, I was just hopping from side to side. I was trying to dodge a belt that made my butt sting every time it met my skin. He whipped me from the waist down. I kept saying sorry, but that didn't work. He didn't stop until he felt like his point was made. As he was whooping me he was yelling at me "you don't do no shit like that", "don't you ever spit on anybody again". After a while I stopped saying "okayyyyyy, I'm sorry" and he stopped. His last words before walking out of the bathroom were "now, shut up before I give you something to cry for."

Eight

By the time I got to high school, I was a huge R. Kelly fan. His music was everything to me, he had some of the best music. I went to his 2007 Double Up concert, where I met my best friend. We both loved his music and that was the start of a lasting friendship. Right before my 15th birthday, R. Kelly started to show up a lot in the press. He was getting ready to go on trial for a tape that allegedly showed him having sex with a minor. I didn't believe it, there was no way I was going to believe that madness. I heard rumors about the tape growing up, but nobody in my family ever talked about it. I heard about it when I went to other people's houses. People knew I was a fan of his in high school and used to say that one day I would get peed on. That was nothing for me to get mad about or give my energy to, I knew R. Kelly was innocent and nobody could tell me any different. When I found out that R. Kelly's trial was going to be in Chicago, I had to go. I wanted to witness everything, I had never been to a trial before, I only watched it on TV, this was a chance for me to see if what I saw on TV was the real thing, besides I wasn't going to miss the chance to see my favorite singer on trial, I didn't care what the trial was for, I thought it would be interesting. On April 1st, 2008 I went to the Cook County Criminal Courts building in Chicago. R. Kelly had a court hearing, I went it. I took the Metra train to the Western stop, then I took the bus to the courthouse. When I got there, there was another fan waiting to see R. Kelly, just like I was. That was the day he noticed me, he spoke to me and thanked me for my support. My 15th birthday was 2 weeks away and the fact that R. Kelly acknowledged me was the best early birthday gift ever.

I was determined to go to R. Kelly's trial, I just wanted to be there and see how everything was going to unfold. At first, I was worried about my mom finding out about me going to his trial, I quickly remembered that I had nothing to worry about, simply because my mom didn't watch the news. My grandma watched the news and kept up with everything that was going on in the world, but her and my mother didn't talk much. The talked on the phone every blue moon. I knew everything was going to work out fine. The trial was nothing like I had expected. It was open to the public anybody was able to attend if they were 18 years old. I never showed an ID and still, I was able to get in, I doubt the ID thing really mattered. I was 15-years-old at R. Kelly's trial. Seeing R. Kelly in the courtroom every day, he didn't seem worried about the drama surrounding him. He was very relaxed and was blowing kisses my way in the courtroom. A few reporters questioned me about it R. Kelly's actions once we were outside of the courtroom. I didn't get tangled up in the media, I was there to see things unfold. It was extremely rare for me to even engage in any sort of conversion with the media. I was just a spectator. Jury selection happened rather fast and the trial was finally set to start and many setbacks. I was ready. The woman that I met on April 1st was also at every court date, just like I was. She showed me where R. Kelly's tour bus used to be parked at, we started to go to the park every morning to talk to him before he went to court, he was always nice to us. On June 13th, 2008 he was found not guilty. Honestly, that's what everyone expected, I don't think anyone had faith in R. Kelly going to jail. My friend and I went to the park where he parked his bus to get our autographs that we were promised at the start of the trial. R. Kelly told us that he was heading downtown to Grand Luxe Café to celebrate the not guilty verdict. That was the last time I saw him for a while.

Nine

May 2009, I posted a status on MySpace about my friend wanting a tattoo never expecting one of R. Kelly's friends to message me. I had been friends with him on MySpace for months before he sent me a message. He messaged me saying "I can do your friend tattoo for her, I have a tattoo shop in Harvey, check out my work." I called my friend and told her that some guy claims to own a tattoo shop. I gave her his information, she checked everything out. She was 24-years-old at the time and I was 16-years-old. She said his shop was real and she wanted to go out there. Once she confirmed things were legit, I gave him my number and we began texting. We met up downtown, go on the Metra train and headed to the tattoo shop. We were about 10 minutes away when I got a text message that read "not at the shop, come to Rob's house" I told my friend "we're being sent off" she asked me "what do you mean?" I asked her "did you call the shop? He's saying he's not there and said to come to Rob house. Who is Rob?" My friend got mad and sad "fuck that, call his ass right now." I called him and his phone went straight to voicemail, at that moment, I was sure that we were being sent off. I texted him and asked, "Who is Rob?" He texted me back right away "R. Kelly. Come to the mansion." My mouth dropped, I couldn't believe was I was reading. My friend grabbed my phone and read the message. The started smiling and said, "Hell yeah, let's go!" I responded, "I don't know where R. Kelly live, how do we know that this is real?" my friend's response was "Bitch, it's R. Kelly, everybody knows where he lives. Shiiiiiiiit, it's only one way to find out, let's go!" We already came to the south suburbs, there was no point in turning back now. I followed her lead and we went to R. Kelly's mansion. One of the security guards came out and asked us who were we there for, we said the shop owners name and we got in. I couldn't believe that we were at R. Kelly's mansion, it didn't seem real. This guy escorted us upstairs to the party. When we walked through the doors, the music was so loud, I couldn't hear myself think, the bass caused my chest to vibrate. There were females everywhere. R. Kelly walked past me and went to the bar, he was drinking what dark liquor. I looked at him and he waved me over. I walked over to the bar, he said "Thank you" I couldn't hear anything else he was saying. He pulled me closer to him and leaned over and said, "give me your phone" I looked at him confused then asked, "am I going to get my phone back?" He laughed in my ear and said "of course", I handed him my phone. I had the Palm Centro, that was the coolest phone ever. He put his number in my phone, then handed me his iPhone for me to put my number in. I looked around for my friend, she was still by the door. I told him that we were leaving. He smiled and nodded his head before taking a sip of his brown liquor. He leaned forward and asked me my age. I told him that I was 19, which was a lie. I was only 16 at the time. Before I could turn around to walk away, he told me to call him when I make it. I said okay then walked over to my friend, who was still by the door. I signaled for her to walk through the door, then I followed. She asked me what happened, I said: "it's too loud, but we exchanged numbers." We left the party and went to the Metra station. I texted Rob and told him that we wouldn't be coming back to his party. He texts back ok. That was only the beginning.

Ten

Rob called me and invited me to his house. I knew that he was going to call me, but I didn't think it would be so soon. I agreed to come over, he told me to make sure I bring a bathing suit, we were going swimming. I told him I will make sure to bring one, he told me to call him when I'm on my way. I told him that I was going to be taking the train, he told me to call him when I get to the train station. Before hanging up, he told me to make sure I didn't tell anybody where I was going. I packed my bathing suit and I told my mom that I was going to my friend's house. My mom didn't question me, she was okay with me going to my "friend's house". She just told me to call when I get there. I assured her that I would call once I got there. A few hours later, I called to let him know that I was at the train station near his house. He told me that someone would be picking me up and that I was to say nothing to the driver. About 5 minutes later a custom painted Chrysler 300 pulled up. This guy got out and said "Jerhonda?" I nodded, remembering not to say anything, and got into the car, he closed the car door, then walked around to the driver side. He got in, turned the radio on and drove off. The ride was so fast, I didn't have time to wrap my head around what was happening. I looked out the window and saw his house; I couldn't believe where I was. We pulled up to the gate and the driver entered a code into the keypad, then the gate opened. For some reason, I didn't feel like I was at R. Kelly's house, I had met him several times at this point, he was just a normal person. He parked the car near a tent on the side of the house. He got out, opened my door, and escorted me to a door on the side of the house. He held the door open for me, I walked ahead of him when I turned around to say "thank you" he was gone. The door that I entered led into the Safari theme pool room. The pool was so nice, it had rainbow illuminating lights, the entire room looked like a jungle, and there was a slide. I called Rob to let him know that I arrived. He said, "put on your bathing suit, I'll be down in 5 minutes." I went into the bathroom near the pool and changed into my bathing suit. 5 minutes turned into 10 minutes, then another 10 minutes went by. When he walked into the pool room he was wearing gray sweats, a white t-shirt, and some white Nike Air Force 1's. The first thing I said is, "I can't swim." He laughed at me as he sat down on a white pool lounge and said, "we're not swimming, you're going to walk for me" I was a bit confused and it showed on my face, he took his shoes off and said, "you're going to walk back and forth like a model." I started walking towards the opposite end of the pool. He told me to "turn around and walk back, every time you walk back you're going to remove a piece of your bathing suit." I literally had on a two-piece, there wasn't much to remove. I walked towards him and removed my top. I turned around to walk back, but he stopped me and told me not to walk back, but to the other end of the pool, but to come to him instead. I walked over to him and he pulled me in for a kiss, he fondled my breast with his left hand, as he gripped my butt with his right hand. He stopped and got up and told me to follow him. I followed him into the game room, this was the same room that he held his party in, a few days ago. He walked me over to a couch, I sat down, and he sat on a couch across from me. My bathing suit top was still in the pool room, all I had on was the bottom piece to my bathing suit. He pulled his penis out and started masturbating. I sat there frozen in time. He told me to relax, then told me to lay back. I did as I was told. He walked over towards me, his pants were at his ankles, his penis was swinging, as he positioned me on the couch and proceeded to perform oral sex on me. I had no feelings about what just happened. I didn't enjoy, I didn't hate it, I was numb to it. After that was done, he pulled his pants up then asked me if I wanted a drink, I said yes. He then jogged over to the pool area and brought me my clothes and purse. Before he went to get me a drink, he told me to follow him into a room. I quickly dressed, then followed him. The room was connected to the game room. The room was a mirror, the walls were mirrors, the ceiling had a mirror on it. It was something I had never seen before. I scanned the room with my eyes and took mental photos. I noticed that there was a bathroom connected to the room, the trim of the door was unique. He told me he would be back, he was going to get me a drink. I sat down on the bed and waited for him to return with my drink. I pulled my phone out and sent out a few text messages. When he came back into the room, he handed me a paper with a phone number on it and told me if I need food or anything to call that number, he then handed me an electric blue looking drink, it was fruity and delicious. He left out and told me he'd be back, he was going to check on the music since he was getting ready for a party later that night. He never left the game room, he tapped on the door and told me to come out, I followed him to the couch with my purse in my hand. We sat down on the couch and talked for a little bit. He did most of the talking, I just listened to all that he had to say. I was looking at him talk, but I couldn't hear anything, all I was thinking was "I need to show him my ID", I went in my purse, pulled out my ID, and handed it to him. He looked at my ID and asked me "what's that supposed to mean?" as he handed my ID back. I replied, "I'm 16". He said, "okay, tell everybody you're 19 and act 21." I had no response to that, he was okay with me being 16-years-old, so I was going to complain. He then invited me to his party. I declined because I suddenly felt sick. I had a headache and didn't feel like doing much of anything. I told him that I didn't feel good and he insisted on me hanging out in music 1 for a little while. He showed me the way to music 1 then he went to prep for his party. It was still early, around 4 PM. I sent out a few text messages, after that, I fell asleep while watching Transformers. I woke up to Rob calling my phone. He told me to go to the studio, I didn't know where the studio was. I thought I was in the studio, it had the instruments and computers there, it was missing microphones though. I told him that I didn't know where the studio was located, he told me that a runner would be there to get me. I waited for that someone to show up. Less than 5 minutes after I spoke with him on the phone, there was a knock at the door. I opened the door and there was a guy standing there, he didn't say anything, he didn't even give a signal. I walked out, he closed the door behind me, then walked in front of me to lead the way. We took a few steps, made two turns and we were at the studio. The studio looked like a log cabin, it was much smaller than music 1. There was a guy in the studio working on an unreleased song. I sat on the couch for about 20 minutes before I called the number that I was given earlier to place a food order. It didn't take long for my McDonald's to come in. Time was really moving fast, I heard the music from where I was, I knew the party had started. I stayed up all night listening to the guy perfect more than 5 new songs. I was bored out of my mind. The guys that were in and out of the studio only talked amongst each other, except the guy who introduced me to Rob. He came into the studio a few times and talked to me. I looked at my phone and it was 6 AM, the party was still going on. I don't understand how people were partying that late. When 7 AM came, I was ready to go. I walked out of the studio, trying to find my way to a bathroom before heading home when I ran into the runner form the day before. He asked me where I was going, I looked around to make sure he was talking to me since he didn't utter a word the day before. I told him that I was looking for a bathroom, then heading home. He gave me directions to the bathroom then told me to make sure I speak with Rob before I go. I didn't think anything of it, I went to use the bathroom then headed back to the studio. I called him, he didn't pick up. I sent him a text message, he didn't respond. He called me back a few minutes later and I told him that I was ready to go home. He insisted on having a runner drive me home, I opted for a ride to the train station instead. He sent a runner to the room to get me and take me to the train. He handed me a white envelope that said "home" on it. I accepted the envelope, got out of the car, and went inside the train station.

Eleven

I didn't see Rob for the next few days. I thought it was
because of my age, but I was wrong. He went to Atlanta for
whatever reason, I never asked him about it. We were
texting and talking on the phone daily while he was away.
When he made it back from Atlanta, he invited me over
that day. He called and told me to call the studio and have
someone pick me up. I turned the ride down and told him
I'd rather take the train to his house. Being on the phone
with him this time, I had butterflies. He was playing his
music in the background, that's what got to me. Only then,
did I realize I was on the phone with R freaking Kelly,
there was no way this was real. I didn't believe. I told him
I'd be there soon then hung up. I had to come back down to
reality, I felt like a superfan. I went to his house on a Friday
afternoon. When I got to the train station near his house, I
called him, and he told me someone would be there soon. I
wasn't expecting him to pick me up, I thought a runner was
going to pick me up. The ride to his house was fast as
usual, I didn't get to finish listening to the Marvin Gaye
song that he had played. We pulled up to the front door and
went straight into the room full of mirrors that were

connected to the game room. I sat down on the bed and Rob looked at me with a straight face and said: "I need you to do something for me." I said, "okay, what do you need?" He asked me if he could trust me when he went on to say as his girlfriend, I should be able to be trusted. I was confused, I didn't know what he was talking about. I knew that I could be trusted, but I didn't know what he needed me to do. From the way he was speaking, pacing, and looking sad, I assumed it was something important. He told me that he would be back. He left out of the room, only to return minutes later with a notepad, a contract, and a pen. He asked me to write letters saying that I stole $250,000 dollars from him and I stole jewelry from him. He then asked if I had any brothers or sisters, I said yes. He told me to write down that he gave me an STD, herpes to be exact. I was supposed to put that my sister put me up to that. As he was telling me what to write, I said: "that's not true though, why would I say that?" His response was "if it's not true, you wouldn't have a problem writing it." I thought about it for a minute then I said, "you're right, I'll write it." He handed me the pen and notepad and I wrote the letter, confessing to things that I didn't do. Once I finished writing the letter, he wanted me to sign a contract saying that I was hired by him and I had to sign another contract that stopped me from discussing anything that happened. The minute the letter was written, and the contracts were signed, things changed. He told me that he was going to train me like a person trains a dog and that I was supposed to follow directions. He explained everything to me, no tight jeans, no dresses, nothing that shows my shape, I had to wear sweats and a t-shirt, if I wanted something I had to ask him, if I needed to use the bathroom I must get his permission, I must address him as Daddy, no looking at men, I'm here to please him, even if that meant pleasing someone else, etc. I guess that was what I signed up for when I didn't read the fine print on those contracts. He put the papers and notepad in his black Nike backpack then told me to undress. I did as I was told. I stripped down to my birthday suit, then he pulled out his iPhone and started taking photos of me. I wasn't comfortable being naked while taking photos. I liked clothes more than anything. He told me to model on the bed while he moved around the room snapping shots. When he was done taking photos, he got undressed and climbed into the bed with me and we talked about sex. I told him that I wanted to be a virgin, but I was sexually abused when I was younger. He looked at me as if he had been waiting his entire life to hear those words. He shared his experience with me about being sexually abused by a man in his old neighborhood and by his old babysitter. We talked about our children for almost two hours. I felt like I knew and understood him. We both had been abused. I felt even closer to him. Later, that night, I lost my virginity to him, though it was nothing like I thought it would be. I had to follow instructions, he directed everything. Back arching and moaning were coached, I was having moaning lessons while having sex. He would tell me when to moan and how loud I should be. I was relieved when it finally was over.

Twelve

A few days later, he was having another party. I found
myself looking for a way to avoid this party. I was tired of
his parties, they were every day, I didn't want to be a part
of that anymore. This man partied entirely too damn much,
and I wasn't up for it. I took myself downstairs to the
basement. I decided to be seen. I was hanging out in the
back near the door. The people there were a lot friendlier.
They interacted with everyone. It was around 3 AM when a
drunk woman and her friend approached the back, where I
was sitting. She sat down right next to me and I
immediately recognized her, she was the girl from the
infamous sex tape. My mouth dropped. I could not believe
that I was sitting next to her, after everything that
happened. It was a shocking revelation. Months ago, people
had teased me at school, saying what happened to her
would be done to me and here she was, sitting right here,
next to me. The runner then said, "Shawn your cab is here",
that confirmed it for me. It truly was her. I headed to the
studio after that. Rob text me and said, "Stay there." I don't
know how he knew anything regarding my whereabouts,
but he did. I sat in the studio for hours. I called to order

food a few times, but no one brought it to me. Rob wasn't answering his phone either. It was now 12 PM. I decided not to wait around any longer. I grabbed my purse then headed out. The runner was sitting at the desk near the door. He told me that I couldn't leave without speaking to Rob first. Initially, I hesitated to speak, though decided against it. I informed him that I couldn't get ahold of Rob, but I needed to go home. He told me to wait in the studio, he would get him for me. I walked back to the studio and sat on the couch. I received a phone call almost immediately after returning. it was Rob. He wanted to know what was going on. I explained to him that I was ready to go home, I needed to shower, brush my teeth, and most importantly, get some sleep. He told me that I could shower, and he had some clothes that I could wear as well as a toothbrush. He gave specific instructions, I was to wait for a runner. the runner would bring me clothes then take me to the bathroom to shower. After that, while I was in the bathroom, I was supposed to leave my clothes outside of the door for the housekeeper to wash and return. When the runner eventually came to get me, he had a new toothbrush, some black sweats, and a white shirt. I was small, the clothes were oversized, yet comfortable, so I didn't complain. After I showered, I went back to the studio. A few hours later my old clothes were dropped off. I went to the bathroom and I changed back into those clothes, discarding the newer ones. I didn't want to go all day without wearing panties and a bra, so I rather put my previous outfit back on since it had been cleaned. I didn't talk to Rob again until 9 AM the next morning. When he called my phone, I was pissed off and demanded that I go home. He apologized and said that he was busy. I complained about staying in the studio for the weekend and told him that I was leaving now. He apologized again and said that he was going to send a runner to take me home, I declined the ride home and told him I'd like a ride to the train station instead. He said "Okay, wh-", I hung up before he was able to finish his sentence. Damn near 30 minutes later the runner came to the studio and handed me a white envelope with $100 in it. Then he took me to the train station. I was relieved to finally be going home. I needed to clear my head. Ultimately, I'd never get the chance to that day. Upon arriving at the station, I was suddenly being taken right back to Rob. I wanted to protest, to ask questions, though I stayed silent, relishing in confusion and frustration. Talking to the runner would only be asking for a punishment. 'If I felt like I ever had even a slight chance of choosing when to go home, the thought had dwindled now. Arriving back at the house, seemingly everything was moving at its typical speed. I awaited judgment, though it didn't come. Oddly, enough, it wouldn't come until three days later. Over the duration of those three days, there was nothing but an uncomfortable feeling in the air. My anger had been replaced by an anxious feeling. I'd see Rob, here and there, though he'd never spoken. Around that third day, I began to put my guard down as he finally spoke to me while inside of music 1. He didn't have much to say, in fact, he just wanted to take my phone away. Before handing my phone over, I asked if I could call my mom to let her know I was going to be on my way home. He told me to call and directed the conversation. I told her that I was going to come home the next day, though I wanted to leave before that, I had to make it work somehow. I gave him my phone when I was done talking to my mom. He powered my phone down and told me to get a new phone after handing me $350 dollars. I asked him how would I get in touch with people? His reply was "That's the point, you don't need to call anybody other than me." I didn't say anything.

Thirteen

I was sitting on the couch in music 1 when he walked in.
Rob sat down on the couch next to me. He asked me if I
was hungry because he was about to order some Chinese
food. He put an order in for our Chinese food as we talked
about sports while we waited for the food. Sometime
during our chowing down, we began to have a
disagreement that turned into a heated argument. I didn't
like the Chicago Bulls, I was a Cleveland Cavaliers fan, the
Chicago Bulls wasn't even my top 10 picks. He didn't
agree with that and tried to force me to like the Chicago
Bulls. I felt this whole argument was ridiculous and told
him that while standing my ground on me NOT like the
Chicago Bulls. I looked at him and he didn't look the same.
I tried to play it off by saying the Chicago Bulls sometimes
played well but his eyes were dark, and he had a blank
expression on his face. I knew this look. This was the kind
of look where you said something sassy to a parent, though
immediately raced to backtrack because you know you'd
hit a button, from the slow head turn and look in their eye.
He got up from the couch and walked in front of me while I

was still sitting. Before I could utter a word, I was suddenly slapped in my face. He slapped me so hard that my face snapped to the side and I toppled over, knocking leftovers onto the floor and beside his feet. I could feel the outline of his fingers that contacted my face, forming on my skin with a sweltering sensation. My eyes welled with tears that threatened to fall. There was a fear that rushed over me. I was scared to look at him, I didn't know what he was going to do next. He was going off saying "That's that stupid shit I was talking about. Your mouth too smart shut the fuck up sometimes." This was a side of him that I never knew existed. The last thing he told me was, "Stop talking so fucking much. Fuck the Cavs!" Then he walked out.

Fourteen

I couldn't believe I got slapped for having an opinion. I learned that I wasn't allowed to have an opinion that night. I can't disagree with anything. I made a mental note to avoid having something like that happen again. I was so shocked that I couldn't cry. My face was still hurting as I spit out chewed food I didn't get the chance to swallow and was surprised didn't fly out of my mouth. What he did wasn't cool. I was going to make sure he knew just how I felt about being slapped. I had some words for him, I was going to give him a piece of my mind. I was going over what I was going to say to him. I was okay with having a disagreement, but I wasn't okay with being hit for not agreeing. A few minutes into my thoughts, he walked back into music 1. He stayed by the door, closing it as he said, "I need you to do something for me." I said, "Okay." Wearily. He looked like his normal self, only in a rush, and with something on his mind. He was holding something on his side, hidden by his shirt, in his sweatpants pocket. It seemed like my initial thoughts of giving him a piece of my mind had went on standstill now as I tried examining him. I didn't want to be hit again. He didn't waste any time before pulling his penis out. I didn't know what to say or think. My face was still burning. He had JUST slapped me, though now he was walking over to the couch with his penis in his hand. Although I didn't know what to say or do, I stared seldom at him, careful of my facial expressions. I was hit for disagreeing, I didn't want to be hit for judging him now. He pulled his pants down to his ankles, he didn't have on any underwear. What was in his pocket, he handed to me. He laid on his back as I stared down at the thick black dildo. He told me it was a 9 inch. Then he told me to walk over by the door. I asked him, "What am I supposed to do with this?" He responded, "Put it in!" I was hoping he wasn't telling me to put it inside of me, I didn't know what I was doing, I had never had that kind of large-sized action before. I didn't even know how or where to begin. Once I made it to the door, I turned around to walk towards him, he was laying on his back with his legs in the air and his pants were still at his ankles. He said, "Put it in." Then it registered in my mind, what he was talking about. I looked at him with uncertainty. He knew I was questioning his request, I allowed curiosity to get the best of me and I said: "I heard when guys do that it means they're ga-". He cut me off before I could finish. He got off the couch so fast, forgetting his pants were at his ankles, he almost fell, but I knew I couldn't laugh. He walked over to me screaming "I'm not fucking gay. What the fuck is wrong with you believing shit like that?" He was coming towards me fast, his eyes were filled with fire, his horns were showing, I knew the devil was about to strike again. I didn't have time to redeem myself before he slapped my face in the same spot, then he backhanded my other cheek. His knuckle came across my right eye. I didn't hold back the tears, I cried. He walked back and told me to "Fucking listen like the dog I'm training you to be." He tripped while going back and fell onto the couch. He laid back down in his position. I was told to crawl towards him on all fours, like a dog. I got down on my knees, barely able to see out of my right eye, the hit left me seeing black spots and I crawled over like a dog towards him, tears still falling from my eyes. When I reached him, he was ready for action? I slowly put the dildo up his anus, he didn't need lube or any assistance. He immediately began to arch his back and moan as I put in more than half of the dildo. He started thrusting his hips, and my arm went limp as the dildo disappeared. What was happening? Had it gone too deep? Had I hurt him? In a breathy tone, he told me to go sit in the chair and watch him, he didn't want me getting involved. He used his left hand to play with his anus as he masturbated with his right hand. It seemed like this lasted forever, him thrusting his hips and rubbing himself, moaning profoundly. Physically I was there, though mentally I had checked out. I felt like I was stuck in neutral. Once he was done pleasuring himself, I quietly told him that I needed to go home tomorrow. Since I no longer had a phone it would be hard for me to continue to lie to my family. He said "Okay, I'll make sure you get there. Don't mention where you've been." And like that, he got himself together and left out. I looked down at the food on the floor, the couch pillows that were unadjusted and felt the hot skin on my cheek, under my fingertips and broke down.

Fifteen

When I made it home, I deleted his phone number. I showered then went to sleep. The next day, I had no intentions to go back to see Rob after that. I did not deserve to be slapped in my face. Just because I'm from Chicago doesn't mean I have to like the Chicago Bulls. What happened after that, it repulsed me to think about and being slapped a second time because I was confused was wrong. Lastly, I wasn't okay with being in a studio for extended periods of time. I went into my mom's room to talk to her. She was getting ready to take my younger siblings to Chuck E. Cheese. It seemed like my mom was always moving. She was always busy with chasing after my younger siblings, keeping our home tidy and making sure the bills were paid. My older sister had a boyfriend now and spent a lot of her time with him. My older brother, whom I was always close with, had ventured off and made a bunch of guy friends he was constantly hanging with now. So really, it was just me, my mother and younger siblings whenever I came home. As we all got ready, I expected my mother to question me. A small part of me did. . . I wanted her to be curious, to peel back my layers and make me expose all that was happening. Though she never did. My mother rarely questioned me about my whereabouts, because when I said I was going to my grandmother's house or to a friend's here in the suburbs, I had to have been telling the truth. Plus, I hadn't given her any reason to doubt me. I suppose because we had spent so many of our years trapped in a house, or constantly looking over our shoulders in the ghetto, now that we lived in the suburbs my mom put her guard down and allowed space for freedom. I decided to add myself to their plans. I spent the entire day with my family, I missed them so much. I hadn't really been seeing them. Before we headed home from Chuck E. Cheese's I told my mom that I lost my phone and would need a replacement. She was okay with me getting another phone on her Sprint line. When we finally made it back home, my stomach was full of pizza and my feet were aching from running after my siblings, I found myself texting a familiar number on my new phone. I texted Rob to let him know that I had another phone, out of the habit of always having to keep him updated, and that I was never coming back. I was his girlfriend and I didn't think that was how girlfriends should be treated. I didn't want to be his girlfriend anymore. Moments after the text was sent, he called my phone from a number that I didn't recognize and apologized for everything. I was firm on not going back to his house until he began to beg me to come back and promised to never hit me again. I felt in my heart that he was truly sorry. He had even sounded as if he was going to cry. He was only human. And as for the dildo, who was I to judge? He explained to me that the male's G-spot was located there. I ultimately accepted his apology, out of guilt, and began to pack my bag. I ended up telling my mother I was spending the night at a friend's house. She was so tired, I barely heard what she said, before rolling over and falling asleep herself. A few hours later I was back at his house, in the same room that he slapped me in. I wasn't at the house long before he came and got me. He took me upstairs to a bedroom. I had never been to this bedroom before. It was on the other side of the house. It was a big bedroom with a beautiful black bedroom set, a sitting area with two chairs and a TV. There was a lot of African culture in the room. He had hand painted African sculptures everywhere, it was beautifully decorated. I sat my overnight bag on the floor and he instructed me to change my clothes. I had to get undressed in front of him. He watched me closely and examined my body as I stripped down. I had to get completely naked. He checked every part of my body and did an internal exam as well, he wanted to make sure that I wasn't having sex with anyone else when I was going home. I felt violated, he had never done this before, his excuse was that he loved me so much, he didn't want me to be with anyone other than him when he wasn't present. I put my sweats on and we both sat on the bed. He looked at me with sad eyes and started telling me about how he watched his mother go through abusive relationships and how his father had abandoned him. He was crying and asking me to forgive him for mistreating me. He said, "I didn't mean any of those things, but I just need you to listen to Daddy. I will never tell you anything wrong. If you listen to me everything will be good." With a heavy, guilt-filled and sympathetic heart, I apologized for not listening and told him, I would listen more. He then said, "You have to gain Daddy's trust back, how do I know I can trust you after that?" I told him that I was trustworthy. He said, "You have to show me I can trust you. Come with Daddy." I followed him to the mirror room that connected to the game room. When we walked in he took all his clothes off and climbed onto the bed. He told me to do the same thing. I removed my clothes, then he told me to go into one of the nightstands and get whatever was inside. I hesitantly pulled out a yellow strap-on dildo. I knew that I couldn't ask any questions, I didn't want to get slapped again. Even though he said it wouldn't happen again, I wanted to avoid all possibilities of being slapped again. I was trying to figure the strap out when he noticed my confusion. He got out of the bed and helped me put it on then told me what to do. He got back on the bed and crawled on all fours and arched his back. I got in the bed. As I penetrated him from behind he moaned, arched his back and masturbated. He told me to call him my "little bitch" and slap his ass. It was uncanny looking at myself in the mirror. What was I doing? When he was at his peak he told to stop and to go in the other drawer and get the other thing out. I pulled the yellow strap out of his anus then I got the dildo out of the drawer. This was a brown dildo. It was bigger than the yellow strap. I handed it to him and he reached behind himself and put it in his anus. I thought I was done and started to remove the strap-on. He told me to leave it on, it was a turn on for him. He told me to get on my knees in front of the bed. He got out of bed as well, the dildo still inserted. I was on my knees facing the bed and he was standing there, masturbating. He told me that my breast was the bullseye. He started jerking harder and harder until he ejaculated on my chest, his semen, hot and sticky running down my breasts. He put his clothes on and told me not to get dressed. Slowly, I stood, feeling less of a human and more of a trash bin as I settled down onto the bed, naked. As I looked up at him, he asked: "What do you think about having sex with another guy?" I said, "I'm not having sex with another guy." He suddenly slapped me so hard I fell off the bed, and onto my knees onto the floor. He started yelling at me saying, "You still don't listen with yo' young ass. Now, you on punishment, you gon' learn to fucking listen." I had my head down, my eyes wide staring at my hands as I struggled to catch the breath he knocked out of me. He walked out of the room and slammed the door.

Sixteen

Three days later, I was still in the mirror room. I hadn't dared to leave the room. I knew I couldn't. I had not eaten since the day that I was put on punishment. I was able to brush my teeth though, luckily. I had a toothbrush that was always in that bathroom. I tried to call Rob again, for the hundredth time it seemed, but he was still ignoring my calls and none of the runners would bring me food. I walked on eggshells all the way to the bedroom that had my overnight bag. Out of habit, I knocked before entering the room. Thankfully it was unlocked. I went inside and grabbed my bag. I tiptoed all the way back to the game room. I was scared that I would be caught and get my ass beat. Once I made it back into the game room, I needed to make it to the shower. I went to the bathroom. I was so scared that I would get caught. I didn't plan to get dressed in the bathroom, it would just be easier for me to just get dressed in the mirror room. I took the fastest shower I had ever taken in my life. After I showered, I felt a lot better, though my stomach felt like it was practically touching my back. I decided that I was going to go downstairs to the basement and find someone to get me some food. I made a bold move and left out of the room. If Rob was gone, I was sure I could at least get something into my system without him knowing. Only thing was, I had no idea where he was. I headed downstairs to the basement. I passed by music 1, the door was opened, I didn't stop. I walked to the desk by the door and saw a new runner. I thought because this was a new runner, that I could easily get away with this. I asked him to do a restaurant run to get me some Harold's Chicken. He asked, "What room are you in?" I told him in a cool, collected tone, the game room, as If I weren't desperate. He said okay. I headed back upstairs, my heart racing. I didn't make it to the top of the stairs before Rob called me. My heart stopped and so did my feet. I answered my phone to him telling me that my food would be coming soon and to be ready for "more" when he gets back, he's on his way to play basketball. I was relieved that I was able to eat, though I wasn't sure what "more" was but I said, "Okay, I'll see you later, Daddy." I saw another young lady in sweats, she walked past me and down the stairs with her head down. I continued up the stairs and got back on my phone. I called my mom and told her that I was at my Grandma's house. She wanted to talk, I had been out for quite some time now, but I rushed her off the phone because someone began to knock at the door. To my surprise, I opened the door to some flowers and a Louis Vuitton box. I knew that was Rob's way of saying sorry. I said, "Thank you," to the runner and closed the door. I opened the box and it was a Louis Vuitton purse. I called him to thank him for my gift. He didn't answer so I sent him a text message. My food came half an hour later. After eating my food, I decided to explore my new-found freedom. Clearly, Rob was no longer mad. I found the theater room. I sat there for all of 15 minutes, before making my way to music 1. The door was still open when I walked over there. Love and Basketball was playing on the TV. I closed the door and watched the movie. Somehow, I ended up falling asleep on the couch. I woke up to Rob calling me around 9AM. He told me to come to his tour bus. I went to the bathroom and brushed my teeth. When I got to tour bus, there was a young girl on the bus performing oral sex on him. I wasn't ready for that, I had no warning or anything. So of course, upon arrival, I was taken aback though had to immediately recover and play it cool. He told me to take off my clothes and join in. As I took my clothes off, he told me that she was around "Since 15 years old." I didn't know what he meant by that because it made no sense. He had the girl and I perform oral sex on one another while he masturbated. I didn't want to participate, but I knew if I didn't he would hit me again, maybe with greater force this time around. When that was over, he had us perform oral on him. Once he ejaculated, we were told to spit hit semen back and forth in each other mouth. I never felt so disgusted. He masturbated more and thrust his hips on the couch as he watched. That's when I noticed that he had a dildo up his anus. I was silently praying and hoping for it to be over. It took him no time to finish. He ended it by ejaculating on our faces and slapping our foreheads with his penis. I was no longer myself.

Seventeen

For the next two days, I stayed in the room. Rob and I
didn't talk much after that. It had to lead me to wonder if
him not speaking much was done purposely because he was
mad at me or something. Had he disliked how me and that
girl performed? Had he sensed I disliked it. My worried
feelings of him would disappear when he finally called.

Rob called my phone and told me to come upstairs to the
game room. I didn't know what to expect. I was trying to
remember if I had done anything that was worthy of a
punishment. I hadn't disobeyed any others that day, he
seemed to have been in a good mood when I saw him
earlier, so I couldn't quite figure it out. I was a bit scared
because I didn't know what to expect, I wasn't trying to be
on his bad side. Besides I wanted my Harold's chicken with
mild sauce. Whatever I did, I was already planning my
apology. I was sorry for being sorry. The walk from Studio
1 to the game room seemed like the longest walk of my
life. By the time I reached the door to the game room, my
palms were sweating. I knocked on the door and waited for

him to open it. Once he did, he simply told me to sit on the couch. I did just that. When Daddy is talking, you must listen. His mood determined rather of not you can ask questions. I sat there, silently- waiting for him to speak. He sat across from me and asked me "Can I trust you?" I said "Yes, you can always trust me" he nodded his head in agreement before saying "I've trusted you with shit I haven't told motherfuckers that have been around me for 20 years. I need to know if I can really trust you?" I felt relieved knowing that I wasn't on his bad side, no punishment for me, but I was curious about what was going on. I reminded him that he can trust me. He then brought up judgment, his next question is "would you ever judge me?" Without hesitation, I said "No, never. I would never judge you, you can trust me." He said okay. Then he got up, opened the door and in walked a familiar face, a familiar guy. He was the same one who invited me to Rob's party. He didn't speak, he just walked over to the couch that Rob was sitting on and sat next to me. I instantly thought, "Oh shit! Rob saw him talk to me in the studio. I know he's about to snap." That wasn't the case. Rob looked at me and smiled. His friend looked at Rob for approval before getting on his knees in front of him. Rob then suddenly removed his penis from his pants. Within a second, his secret lover began to give him head. Yes, I was watching as Rob received oral from another man. What was more shocking to me was that his secret lover was moaning and humming as he did it. I thought to myself, Rob taught me how to do that same thing. Rob started rubbing his friend's head as he moaned in pleasure. After a few seconds of this, he tapped his secret lover on the shoulder, letting him know that was enough. I didn't know what to expect. I continued to watch as the two then got up and walked behind the couch. Rob's secret lover undressed from the bottom down. That was when Rob bent him over, after doing the exact same, and inserted his penis into his friend's anus. I continued to watch with a good poker face though I was stirring inside. I was in shock and in disbelief about what I was seeing. I sat there, bewildered with a straight face as they escaped into ecstasy, seemingly forgetting my presence. I couldn't judge him and to see him have sex with a man couldn't change my view of him. Daddy was a lover of people; no judgment could be passed.

Eighteen

Leaving wasn't easy for me, but I knew that I had to get out
of there. I didn't want to be in that situation anymore. The
night I left, I felt it coming. Things just felt different. Rob
picked me up from the train station. He was in a good
mood. It was his birthday month and he was getting ready
for a party, Chicago winters are brutal, but he still had a lot
of people coming to celebrate him. It took longer than usual
to get to his house, due to the weather. When we arrived at
his house, he walked around and opened the car door for
me and carried my bag. I followed him to the game room. I
took my coat off and sat on the couch. We had a brief
conversation about his party. I really wasn't in the mood to
go, but I agreed to be there, only because it was his
birthday party. I'm not a fan of his parties, honestly. He
received a phone call and left out of the room. When he
returned to the room, I didn't hear him come in, I was too
wrapped up in my phone. I was texting my friends to make
sure they covered for me. I told my friends about him, they
knew where I was really going. He caught me on my phone
and assumed that I was texting a guy. I don't know what

gave him that impression. He asked me who was I talking to. I quickly stated that I was talking to a friend, but he wasn't buying it. I was being honest, but he already had his doubt. He walked over to me, snatched my phone out of my hand, and slapped me in my face. I knew this wasn't going to be good. I tried to walk away, but he pushed me against the wall and choked me. As if that was enough, he decided to spit in my face. Afterward, he told me to put my head down in shame. I did just that and then came the lecture. I knew he was going too much more, his party was hours away. He had his image to protect. So, I sat there and listened to him call me a stupid bitch and talk about how my family disowned be due to my stupidity. I was called everything but my name. I apologized for whatever he felt like I did. He didn't care, he got up and left the room. He returned less than 5 minutes later and apologized. He blamed it on him not wanting to share me with anybody. . . A bunch of crap that I had already heard. When he changed the subject and mentioned his party, I knew I had a chance to get out of there. How many times was I going to be slapped around? I contemplated staying there because I really loved him, but I knew it wasn't worth it. I was beating myself because I knew he wasn't a bad person, he just had bad days. Over the course of 8 months I lived a repetitive life; sleep, eat, sex. I was always on punishment, being locked in the room. He coached me on everything. Answers to potential questions were rehearsed. I was manipulated, abandoned, and starved several times. I was forced to have sex with women that I didn't want to have sex with, I was being physically abused, I always got slapped, I wasn't allowed to have my phone around him, I had to keep his secrets, watch gay porn, watch him have sex with a man, etc. I was recorded every time we had sex; I never gave consent. The more that I thought about it the more I wanted to leave. I had no freedom, I couldn't do anything. I told him I was still going to be there, I just needed to get dressed. He told me what to wear. I told him that my heels were at my uncle's house. Rob knew that I had an uncle who lived within walking distance of him. I didn't talk to my uncle much, that's what he didn't know. He trusted me with everything; I always came back whenever I left, I never stayed out longer than expected, and I knew some of his darkest secrets, according to him. He told me to hurry up and get my shoes. I know he agreed because he loved to see me in those heels. When I left, I only took my cell phone and the cash I had on hand. I walked to the train and never went back. I would probably still be with him if it wasn't for him spitting in my face.

That made me feel like the scum of the earth, that was something I couldn't accept under any circumstances.

Nineteen

Once I left I told everything that happened. I told my sister first, then I told my mom. They didn't believe it, the fact that it happened in plain sight is what they couldn't understand. How was I able to get to his house, be gone for weeks at a time, and nobody knew anything about it? It wasn't that hard to get away, especially with my mom being busy with my younger siblings. I was a middle child; therefore, I was always looked over. Whenever I said I was going somewhere, no one would investigate it, I just had to say something. I had a good relationship with my mom, but it wasn't the best. With my dad being incarcerated and my mom not paying much attention to me, I looked for love in the wrong places. It all ended with a $1.5 million-dollar settlement, mental scars, and a lifelong STD (herpes) that I can't get rid of. I stopped accepting money from Rob in August of 2017 when I went public and told my story. I've never felt so free in my life. Seeing a family come forward about Rob having their daughter in an abusive cult, I knew I had to speak up. I have three daughters and I can't imagine what they're going through. I know firsthand what their daughter is experiencing. I never want my girls to grow up and think that abuse is okay if you're getting paid. Abuse is NOT okay. At one point in time, I believed Rob when he told me that my family didn't love me. I always felt abandoned, I felt like something was missing. When I became Rob's girlfriend, things seemed to be going well, until I made him mad. Whenever I made him mad, he became a different person. I also believed it was my fault, I was the reason for the abuse. It had gotten to the point where I took Rob's advice and convinced my mom to allow me to finish high school online, that's how I got around going back into a physical school.

Silenced

I've never gone to counseling; I did meditation, I enjoy meditating. Sexual abuse is a serious thing within the black community. Through my nonprofit organization, I learned that it wasn't just my family who refused to speak on sexual abuse, there were people in every black family that I had encountered who refused to speak about it. For some reason, black women who have been sexually abused are not allowed to talk about it. When you bring up sexual abuse; nobody wants to speak on it. It happens often among black families. There's that creepy uncle who touches the little girls and instead of speaking out, stepping up, and protecting young black girls, that creepy uncle is often used as a scare tactic. Many times, I've heard "keep acting up, I'm going to send you over uncle (insert name) house" knowing that that uncle is a known pedophile in the family. I've heard my own family members use scare tactics such as that. When it comes to black families if you speak out against a predator in the family, you're the one that's disowned, you're looked at differently, at that point you're nothing more than a shit starter and you can't be trusted. There is no help or support for the brave survivors who wish to come forward, so a lot of them don't. They continue to live in the shadows, hug their predators, and love their rapist. Our voices are not heard, we must be strong, we're forced to move on.

Believe

My life after abuse has been AMAZING, I couldn't ask for a better life. Starting over for me was the easy part, trusting someone after all that I had been through was the hard part. My husband was patient, genuine, loving, and persistent. My sister was my shoulder to cry on and gave advice every time I needed it and pushed me to keep going. My children are everything to me, they are my reason. What I went through inspired me to help others. Now, I'm a psychology major, I'm one semester closer to my doctorate degree. I spend a lot of time at abuse shelters, supporting abuse victims and survivors. I also have a non-profit organization: alifebeyondabuse.org

Love yourself all ways, always.

A Closer Look

Music 1

My food inside of music 1

The mirror above the bed

Music 1 with Snow (Rob's dog)

Mirror room

2. After telling R. Kelly you were 16, did you have vaginal intercourse with him more than one time? Answer (YES)

3. In July of 2009, did R. Kelly have you write out some letters indicating your dishonesty and that your family was using you to set him up? Answer (YES)

Page 3

Inc.

Jerhonda M. Johnson – cont.

Test Results – cont.

4. On Saturday, January 23, 2010, did R. Kelly slap, choke, and spit on you when he questioned your sexual fidelity with others besides himself? Answer (YES)

There were no significant physiological responses indicative of deception throughout her polygraph records on the previously listed questions.

It is the opinion of this examiner, based upon an analysis of her polygraph records, that she is truthful in her answers to the previously listed questions.

Respectfully submitted,

Polygraph results

("Johnson") and Robert Kelly ("Kelly") are presently engaged in disputes concerning the existence and nature of their past relationship, if any. Johnson and Kelly have determined to settle and resolve any and all disputes between them. Therefore, Johnson and Kelly, agree as follows:

1. Kelly enters into this Confidential Settlement Agreement and Release ("Agreement") without any admission of liability of or wrong-doing, and Kelly expressly denies engaging in any improper or wrongful conduct of any type or manner.

2. Kelly will pay to Johnson a total settlement consideration of

$1,500,000.00, which shall hereinafter be referred to as the "Settlement Proceeds". The Settlement Proceeds will be paid according to the following schedule:

   a. $250,000.00 payable by within 48 hours of 2/17/10 and of execution of this Agreement by plaintiff by wire transfer deposited into the account of Susan E. Loggans & Associates, PC.

   b. $250,000.00 payable within 14 days after 2/17/10 and Execution of this Agreement by wire transfer deposited into the account of Susan E. Loggans & Associates, PC.

CPSIA information can be obtained
at www.ICGtesting.com
Printed in the USA
LVHW02s0231041018
592362LV00017B/672/P